ZIMBABWE COOKBOOK

Traditional Recipes from Zimbabwe

LIAM LUXE

Copyright © 2024 Liam Luxe

All rights reserved.

CONTENTS

INTRODUCTION i

STARTERS AND APPETIZERS 1
    Dovi (Peanut Soup) 1
    Muboora (Pumpkin Leaves with Peanuts) 2
    Huku neDovi (Chicken with Peanut Sauce) 3
    Mazondo (Beef Trotters Stew) 4
    Chibage neNyama (Butternut and Meat Stew) 5
    Boerewors Rolls with Sadza Fries 6
    Bota (Tripe and Vegetable Stew) 7
    Madora (Fried Caterpillars) 8
    Mapopo Candy (Guava Candy) 9
    Sadza Cakes with Tomato Gravy 10

MAIN COURSES - MEAT 12
    Nyama Choma (Grilled Meat) 12
    Dovi la Piri-Piri (Peanut and Peri-Peri Chicken) 13
    Mopane Worms Stir-Fry 14
    Boerewors Rolls with Chakalaka 15
    Zambezi Bream with Nhedzi (Wild Mushrooms) 17
    Game Meat Skewers 18
    Beef and Vegetable Bobotie 19
    Kombi Stew (Mixed Meat Stew) 20
    Kapenta with Sadza 22
    Dikgobe (Tripe and Peanut Stew) 23

MAIN COURSES - VEGETARIAN 25

Taka-Taka (Okra and Tomato Stew) 25

Nhopi (Sweet Potato and Peanut Butter Stew) 26

Mutakura (Pumpkin and Peanut Butter Stew) 27

Chakalaka (Spicy Vegetable Relish) 29

Muriwo Unedovi (Greens with Peanut Sauce) 30

Bambara Nut and Vegetable Curry 31

Mazhanje Cake (Baobab Fruit Cake) 32

Pumpkin and Bean Stew 33

Sadza Patties with Chibage (Butternut) Sauce 35

Muboora and Mushroom Pilaf 36

SIDE DISHES 39

Sadza (Cornmeal Porridge) 39

Nhedzi naDovi (Wild Mushrooms with Peanut Butter) 40

Huku neDovi Sadza (Chicken with Peanut Sauce and Cornmeal) 41

Morogo (Wild Spinach) 43

Dovi-Maputi (Peanut Brittle) 44

Muboora and Butternut Fritters 45

Mahewu Bread (Fermented Maize Drink Bread) 46

Pumpkin Fritters 47

Nyimo (Bambara Nut) Salad 48

Chibage (Butternut) and Potato Mash 49

BREADS AND GRAINS 51

Sadza Loaf 51

Bota-Bota (Tripe Porridge) 52

Mahewu (Fermented Maize Drink)	53
Mupunga neNyama (Rice and Meat)	54
Muboora Muffins	55
Sorghum and Millet Porridge	57
Pumpkin Bread	58
Tsunga (Finger Millet) Pancakes	59
Sadza Cakes with Greens	60
Bambara Nut Porridge	62
DESSERTS AND SWEETS	**64**
Maheu Ice Cream	64
Mapopo (Guava) Sorbet	65
Dovi Pudding	66
Mbatata (Sweet Potato) Pie	67
Banana Fritters	69
Maziwa Malambe (Condensed Milk Fudge)	70
Mahewu Smoothie	71
Mutakura (Pumpkin) Doughnuts	72
Chibage (Butternut) Muffins	74
Madora (Caterpillar) Chocolate Truffles	75
MEASUREMENT CONVERSIONS	**77**

INTRODUCTION

This book is all about the tasty and diverse food from Zimbabwe. It's like taking a trip to Zimbabwe without leaving your kitchen. In this book, you'll find recipes that show the amazing flavors of Zimbabwe's food. From delicious stews with peanuts to spicy chicken, each recipe is a special part of Zimbabwe's food story. People in Zimbabwe use ingredients like maize, sorghum, pumpkin, and different meats to create tasty meals.
These recipes will help you to make Zimbabwean food in your own kitchen. Imagine the smells and sounds of a Zimbabwean kitchen right in your home.
Happy cooking!

STARTERS AND APPETIZERS

DOVI (PEANUT SOUP)

Servings: 4

Time: 45 minutes

Ingredients:

- 1 cup peanuts, ground
- 1 onion, finely chopped
- 2 tomatoes, diced
- 2 cloves garlic, minced
- 1 teaspoon curry powder
- 1 teaspoon paprika
- 1 tablespoon vegetable oil
- 4 cups vegetable or chicken broth

- Salt and pepper to taste
- Chopped fresh cilantro for garnish

Instructions:

1. Heat vegetable oil in a pot over medium heat.
2. Sauté chopped onions until golden brown.
3. Add minced garlic and cook until fragrant.
4. Stir in ground peanuts, curry powder, and paprika.
5. Cook for 3-5 minutes, stirring constantly.
6. Add diced tomatoes and cook until they soften.
7. Pour in the broth, bring to a boil, then reduce heat to simmer.
8. Allow the soup to simmer for 20-25 minutes.
9. Season with salt and pepper to taste.
10. Serve hot, garnished with chopped fresh cilantro.

MUBOORA (PUMPKIN LEAVES WITH PEANUTS)

Servings: 4

Time: 30 minutes

Ingredients:

- 1 bunch pumpkin leaves, washed and chopped
- 1 cup peanuts, roasted and crushed
- 1 onion, finely chopped
- 2 tomatoes, chopped
- 2 tablespoons vegetable oil
- 1 teaspoon ground cayenne pepper (optional)
- Salt to taste

Instructions:

1. Heat vegetable oil in a pan over medium heat.
2. Sauté chopped onions until translucent.
3. Add chopped tomatoes and cook until soft.
4. Stir in crushed peanuts and mix well.
5. Add pumpkin leaves to the mixture.
6. Cook for about 10-15 minutes until the leaves are tender.
7. If desired, sprinkle ground cayenne pepper for added spice.
8. Season with salt to taste.
9. Stir thoroughly and cook for an additional 2-3 minutes.
10. Serve hot as a flavorful side dish.

HUKU NEDOVI (CHICKEN WITH PEANUT SAUCE)

Servings: 4

Time: 50 minutes

Ingredients:

- 1 whole chicken, cut into pieces
- 1 cup peanuts, ground
- 1 onion, finely chopped
- 2 tomatoes, diced
- 3 cloves garlic, minced
- 1 teaspoon ground coriander
- 1 teaspoon paprika
- 2 tablespoons vegetable oil
- 2 cups chicken broth
- Salt and pepper to taste

- Chopped fresh parsley for garnish

Instructions:

1. In a large pot, heat vegetable oil over medium heat.
2. Brown chicken pieces on all sides until golden.
3. Remove chicken from the pot and set aside.
4. In the same pot, sauté chopped onions until soft.
5. Add minced garlic and cook until fragrant.
6. Stir in ground peanuts, ground coriander, and paprika.
7. Cook for 3-5 minutes, stirring constantly.
8. Add diced tomatoes and cook until they break down.
9. Place the browned chicken back into the pot.
10. Pour in chicken broth, bring to a boil, then reduce heat and simmer for 30 minutes.
11. Season with salt and pepper to taste.
12. Garnish with chopped fresh parsley before serving.

MAZONDO (BEEF TROTTERS STEW)

Servings: 4

Time: 2 hours

Ingredients:

- 1 kg beef trotters, cleaned and cut
- 1 onion, finely chopped
- 2 tomatoes, diced
- 3 cloves garlic, minced
- 1 tablespoon tomato paste
- 2 tablespoons vegetable oil
- 2 teaspoons ground cumin

- 2 teaspoons ground coriander
- 1 teaspoon paprika
- Salt and pepper to taste
- Fresh cilantro for garnish

Instructions:

1. In a large pot, heat vegetable oil over medium heat.
2. Sauté chopped onions until golden brown.
3. Add minced garlic and cook until fragrant.
4. Stir in diced tomatoes and tomato paste, cook until tomatoes break down.
5. Add beef trotters to the pot, stirring to coat with the tomato mixture.
6. Season with ground cumin, ground coriander, paprika, salt, and pepper.
7. Pour enough water to cover the trotters and bring to a boil.
8. Reduce heat, cover, and simmer for 1.5 to 2 hours until trotters are tender.
9. Check the seasoning and adjust if needed.
10. Garnish with fresh cilantro before serving.

CHIBAGE NENYAMA (BUTTERNUT AND MEAT STEW)

Servings: 4

Time: 1 hour

Ingredients:

- 500g beef, cubed

- 1 butternut squash, peeled and diced
- 1 onion, finely chopped
- 2 tomatoes, chopped
- 3 cloves garlic, minced
- 2 tablespoons vegetable oil
- 1 teaspoon ground cinnamon
- 1 teaspoon ground nutmeg
- Salt and pepper to taste
- Fresh parsley for garnish

Instructions:

1. In a large pot, heat vegetable oil over medium heat.
2. Sauté chopped onions until soft.
3. Add minced garlic and cook until fragrant.
4. Add cubed beef and brown on all sides.
5. Stir in chopped tomatoes and cook until they soften.
6. Add diced butternut squash to the pot.
7. Season with ground cinnamon, ground nutmeg, salt, and pepper.
8. Pour in enough water to cover the ingredients.
9. Bring to a boil, then reduce heat, cover, and simmer for 30-40 minutes until meat is tender.
10. Check the seasoning and adjust if needed.
11. Garnish with fresh parsley before serving.

BOEREWORS ROLLS WITH SADZA FRIES

Servings: 4

Time: 30 minutes

Ingredients:

- 4 boerewors sausages
- 4 hot dog buns
- 2 cups sadza (cornmeal porridge), cooled and set
- 1 cup all-purpose flour
- 2 eggs, beaten
- Vegetable oil for frying
- Salt and pepper to taste
- Tomato sauce or relish for serving

Instructions:

1. Grill or pan-fry boerewors sausages until cooked through.
2. Split the hot dog buns and warm them on the grill or in a toaster.
3. Cut the sadza into fry-like shapes.
4. In a bowl, season the flour with salt and pepper.
5. Dip the sadza fries into the beaten eggs, then coat with the seasoned flour.
6. Heat vegetable oil in a pan and fry the sadza fries until golden brown.
7. Place the grilled boerewors sausages in the buns.
8. Serve the Boerewors Rolls with a side of crispy Sadza Fries.
9. Add a dollop of tomato sauce or relish on top.

BOTA (TRIPE AND VEGETABLE STEW)

Servings: 4

Time: 2 hours

Ingredients:

- 500g tripe, cleaned and cut
- 1 onion, finely chopped
- 2 tomatoes, diced
- 3 cloves garlic, minced
- 1 cup mixed vegetables (carrots, peas, and beans)
- 2 tablespoons vegetable oil
- 1 teaspoon ground turmeric
- 1 teaspoon ground coriander
- Salt and pepper to taste
- Fresh parsley for garnish

Instructions:

1. In a large pot, heat vegetable oil over medium heat.
2. Sauté chopped onions until golden brown.
3. Add minced garlic and cook until fragrant.
4. Add cleaned and cut tripe to the pot, stirring to coat with the onion mixture.
5. Pour in enough water to cover the tripe and bring to a boil.
6. Reduce heat, cover, and simmer for 1.5 to 2 hours until tripe is tender.
7. Stir in diced tomatoes and mixed vegetables.
8. Season with ground turmeric, ground coriander, salt, and pepper.
9. Continue to simmer for an additional 15-20 minutes until vegetables are cooked.
10. Check the seasoning and adjust if needed.
11. Garnish with fresh parsley before serving.

MADORA (FRIED CATERPILLARS)

Servings: 4

Time: 20 minutes

Ingredients:

- 2 cups madora (caterpillars), cleaned
- 2 tablespoons vegetable oil
- Salt and pepper to taste
- Lemon wedges for serving (optional)

Instructions:

1. In a pan, heat vegetable oil over medium heat.
2. Add cleaned madora to the pan.
3. Fry the caterpillars until golden brown and crispy.
4. Sprinkle with salt and pepper to taste.
5. Remove from the pan and place on a paper towel to drain excess oil.
6. Serve immediately with lemon wedges on the side if desired.

MAPOPO CANDY (GUAVA CANDY)

Servings: Varies

Time: 3 hours

Ingredients:

- 4 cups guava pulp, seeds removed
- 2 cups granulated sugar
- 1 tablespoon lemon juice

Instructions:

1. In a blender, puree the guava pulp until smooth.
2. Strain the puree to remove seeds, yielding a smooth guava liquid.
3. In a wide, heavy-bottomed pan, combine the guava liquid, sugar, and lemon juice.
4. Cook the mixture over medium heat, stirring continuously until the sugar dissolves.
5. Continue to simmer the mixture, stirring frequently, until it thickens to a candy-like consistency. This may take about 2-3 hours.
6. Once the mixture thickens and turns a deeper color, remove it from the heat.
7. Pour the thickened guava mixture into a greased tray or mold.
8. Allow it to cool and set at room temperature or in the refrigerator.
9. Once set, cut the guava candy into bite-sized pieces.

SADZA CAKES WITH TOMATO GRAVY

Servings: 4

Time: 45 minutes

Ingredients: *For Sadza Cakes:*

- 2 cups sadza (cornmeal porridge), cooled
- 1 cup cooked mixed vegetables (peas, carrots, and corn)
- 2 tablespoons vegetable oil
- Salt to taste

For Tomato Gravy:

- 4 tomatoes, chopped
- 1 onion, finely chopped
- 2 tablespoons vegetable oil
- 1 teaspoon sugar
- Salt and pepper to taste
- Fresh cilantro for garnish

Instructions: *For Sadza Cakes:*

1. In a bowl, mix the cooled sadza with cooked mixed vegetables.
2. Shape the mixture into small cakes.
3. Heat vegetable oil in a pan over medium heat.
4. Fry the sadza cakes until golden brown on both sides.
5. Sprinkle with salt to taste.
6. Remove from the pan and set aside.

For Tomato Gravy:

1. In the same pan, heat vegetable oil over medium heat.
2. Sauté chopped onions until soft.
3. Add chopped tomatoes and cook until they break down.
4. Stir in sugar, salt, and pepper.
5. Cook the mixture until it thickens into a gravy consistency.
6. Serve the Sadza Cakes with Tomato Gravy, garnished with fresh cilantro.

MAIN COURSES - MEAT

NYAMA CHOMA (GRILLED MEAT)

Servings: 4

Time: 1 hour (plus marinating time)

Ingredients:

- 1 kg beef or lamb, cut into chunks
- 1 onion, finely chopped
- 2 cloves garlic, minced
- 2 tablespoons vegetable oil
- 1 teaspoon ground coriander
- 1 teaspoon paprika
- Salt and pepper to taste
- Fresh lemon wedges for serving

Instructions:

1. In a bowl, mix chopped onions, minced garlic, vegetable oil, ground coriander, paprika, salt, and pepper to create a marinade.
2. Coat the meat chunks with the marinade, ensuring each piece is well covered.
3. Cover the bowl and let it marinate in the refrigerator for at least 2 hours or overnight for richer flavor.
4. Preheat the grill or barbecue to medium-high heat.
5. Thread the marinated meat onto skewers.
6. Grill the meat skewers for about 10-15 minutes, turning occasionally, until cooked to your desired level of doneness.
7. Remove from the grill and let it rest for a few minutes.
8. Serve the Nyama Choma hot, with fresh lemon wedges on the side.

DOVI LA PIRI-PIRI (PEANUT AND PERI-PERI CHICKEN)

Servings: 4

Time: 1 hour

Ingredients:

- 1 whole chicken, cut into pieces
- 1 cup peanuts, ground
- 2 onions, finely chopped
- 3 tomatoes, diced
- 3 cloves garlic, minced
- 2 tablespoons vegetable oil

- 1 tablespoon peri-peri sauce (adjust to taste)
- 1 teaspoon ground cumin
- 1 teaspoon paprika
- Salt and pepper to taste
- Fresh cilantro for garnish

Instructions:

1. In a large pot, heat vegetable oil over medium heat.
2. Sauté chopped onions until golden brown.
3. Add minced garlic and cook until fragrant.
4. Stir in ground peanuts, peri-peri sauce, ground cumin, and paprika.
5. Cook for 3-5 minutes, stirring constantly.
6. Add diced tomatoes and cook until they break down.
7. Place the chicken pieces in the pot, ensuring they are coated with the peanut mixture.
8. Pour in enough water to cover the chicken, bring to a boil, then reduce heat and simmer for 30-40 minutes until chicken is cooked through.
9. Season with salt and pepper to taste.
10. Garnish with fresh cilantro before serving.

MOPANE WORMS STIR-FRY

Servings: 4

Time: 30 minutes

Ingredients:

- 2 cups dried mopane worms, rehydrated
- 1 onion, finely chopped

- 2 tomatoes, diced
- 3 cloves garlic, minced
- 2 tablespoons vegetable oil
- 1 teaspoon ground chili powder (adjust to taste)
- Salt and pepper to taste
- Fresh coriander for garnish

Instructions:

1. Rehydrate dried mopane worms according to package instructions.
2. In a pan, heat vegetable oil over medium heat.
3. Sauté chopped onions until translucent.
4. Add minced garlic and cook until fragrant.
5. Stir in rehydrated mopane worms and cook for 5-7 minutes.
6. Add diced tomatoes to the pan and cook until they soften.
7. Sprinkle ground chili powder, salt, and pepper over the mixture.
8. Stir-fry for an additional 5-8 minutes until the worms are crispy.
9. Adjust seasoning to taste.
10. Garnish with fresh coriander before serving.

BOEREWORS ROLLS WITH CHAKALAKA

Servings: 4

Time: 30 minutes

Ingredients: *For Boerewors Rolls:*

- 4 boerewors sausages
- 4 hot dog buns
- 1 onion, thinly sliced
- Vegetable oil for grilling

For Chakalaka:

- 1 can baked beans in tomato sauce
- 1 onion, finely chopped
- 1 bell pepper, diced
- 2 tomatoes, chopped
- 2 tablespoons vegetable oil
- 1 teaspoon curry powder
- 1 teaspoon paprika
- Salt and pepper to taste
- Fresh cilantro for garnish

Instructions: *For Boerewors Rolls:*

1. Grill boerewors sausages until cooked through.
2. Split the hot dog buns and lightly toast them on the grill.
3. In a pan, sauté thinly sliced onions until caramelized.
4. Place grilled boerewors sausages in the buns.
5. Top with caramelized onions.

For Chakalaka:

1. In a separate pan, heat vegetable oil over medium heat.
2. Sauté chopped onions until soft.
3. Add diced bell pepper and cook until slightly tender.
4. Stir in chopped tomatoes, curry powder, and paprika.
5. Pour in baked beans in tomato sauce.
6. Simmer the mixture for 10-15 minutes.
7. Season with salt and pepper to taste.

8. Serve the Boerewors Rolls with a generous spoonful of Chakalaka.
9. Garnish with fresh cilantro before serving.

ZAMBEZI BREAM WITH NHEDZI (WILD MUSHROOMS)

Servings: 4

Time: 45 minutes

Ingredients:

- 4 Zambezi bream fillets
- 2 cups nhedzi (wild mushrooms), cleaned and sliced
- 1 onion, finely chopped
- 2 tomatoes, diced
- 3 cloves garlic, minced
- 2 tablespoons vegetable oil
- 1 teaspoon ground paprika
- 1 teaspoon dried thyme
- Salt and pepper to taste
- Fresh parsley for garnish

Instructions:

1. In a pan, heat vegetable oil over medium heat.
2. Sauté chopped onions until golden brown.
3. Add minced garlic and cook until fragrant.
4. Stir in diced tomatoes and cook until they break down.
5. Add sliced wild mushrooms (nhedzi) to the pan and cook until they release their moisture.

6. Push the mushrooms to the side and place Zambezi bream fillets in the pan.
7. Season the fish with ground paprika, dried thyme, salt, and pepper.
8. Cook the bream fillets for 4-5 minutes on each side or until they are cooked through.
9. Ensure the mushrooms are cooked, and the flavors meld together.
10. Garnish with fresh parsley before serving.

GAME MEAT SKEWERS

Servings: 4

Time: 1 hour (plus marinating time)

Ingredients:

- 500g mixed game meat (venison, buffalo, or any preferred game), cubed
- 1 onion, finely chopped
- 2 tablespoons vegetable oil
- 2 tablespoons soy sauce
- 1 tablespoon honey
- 2 cloves garlic, minced
- 1 teaspoon dried oregano
- Salt and pepper to taste
- Wooden skewers, soaked in water

Instructions:

1. In a bowl, mix chopped onions, vegetable oil, soy sauce, honey, minced garlic, dried oregano, salt, and pepper to create a marinade.
2. Add cubed game meat to the marinade, ensuring each piece is well coated.
3. Cover the bowl and let it marinate in the refrigerator for at least 1 hour or overnight for enhanced flavor.
4. Preheat the grill or barbecue to medium-high heat.
5. Thread the marinated game meat onto the soaked wooden skewers.
6. Grill the skewers for about 8-10 minutes, turning occasionally, until the meat is cooked to your desired level of doneness.
7. Remove from the grill and let them rest for a few minutes.
8. Serve the Game Meat Skewers hot.

BEEF AND VEGETABLE BOBOTIE

Servings: 4

Time: 1 hour

Ingredients:

- 500g ground beef
- 1 onion, finely chopped
- 2 carrots, grated
- 1 zucchini, grated
- 2 tablespoons vegetable oil
- 2 tablespoons curry powder
- 1 teaspoon ground cinnamon
- 1 teaspoon ground turmeric

- 2 slices white bread, soaked in milk
- 2 eggs, beaten
- 1 cup milk
- Salt and pepper to taste
- Fresh coriander for garnish

Instructions:

1. Preheat the oven to 180°C (350°F).
2. In a pan, heat vegetable oil over medium heat.
3. Sauté chopped onions until golden brown.
4. Add grated carrots and zucchini, cooking until they are soft.
5. Add ground beef to the pan, breaking it apart with a spoon, and cook until browned.
6. Stir in curry powder, ground cinnamon, and ground turmeric.
7. In a separate bowl, mash the soaked bread with a fork.
8. Add the beaten eggs and mix well.
9. Combine the bread mixture with the cooked beef and vegetables.
10. Transfer the mixture to a baking dish, spreading it evenly.
11. In a separate bowl, whisk together milk, salt, and pepper.
12. Pour the milk mixture over the beef and vegetable mixture.
13. Bake in the preheated oven for 35-40 minutes or until the top is golden and set.
14. Garnish with fresh coriander before serving.

KOMBI STEW (MIXED MEAT STEW)

Servings: 4

Time: 2 hours

Ingredients:

- 500g beef, cubed
- 300g chicken pieces
- 200g pork, diced
- 1 onion, finely chopped
- 3 tomatoes, diced
- 3 cloves garlic, minced
- 2 tablespoons vegetable oil
- 1 teaspoon ground coriander
- 1 teaspoon paprika
- 1 teaspoon dried thyme
- 2 bay leaves
- 4 cups beef or chicken broth
- Salt and pepper to taste
- Fresh parsley for garnish

Instructions:

1. In a large pot, heat vegetable oil over medium heat.
2. Sauté chopped onions until golden brown.
3. Add minced garlic and cook until fragrant.
4. Add cubed beef, chicken pieces, and diced pork to the pot.
5. Brown the meat on all sides.
6. Stir in diced tomatoes, ground coriander, paprika, dried thyme, and bay leaves.
7. Pour in beef or chicken broth, bringing the stew to a boil.
8. Reduce heat, cover, and simmer for 1.5 to 2 hours until the meat is tender.
9. Season with salt and pepper to taste.

10. Remove bay leaves before serving.
11. Garnish with fresh parsley.

KAPENTA WITH SADZA

Servings: 4

Time: 45 minutes

Ingredients:

- 2 cups kapenta (dried small fish)
- 2 cups sadza (cornmeal porridge)
- 1 onion, finely chopped
- 2 tomatoes, diced
- 3 cloves garlic, minced
- 2 tablespoons vegetable oil
- 1 teaspoon ground paprika
- 1 teaspoon dried oregano
- Salt and pepper to taste
- Fresh lemon wedges for serving

Instructions:

1. Rinse kapenta thoroughly under cold water to remove excess salt.
2. In a pan, heat vegetable oil over medium heat.
3. Sauté chopped onions until translucent.
4. Add minced garlic and cook until fragrant.
5. Stir in diced tomatoes, ground paprika, and dried oregano.
6. Add kapenta to the pan, tossing to coat with the onion and tomato mixture.

7. Cook for 5-7 minutes until the kapenta is heated through.
8. Meanwhile, prepare sadza according to package instructions.
9. Season the kapenta mixture with salt and pepper to taste.
10. Serve the kapenta over a bed of sadza.
11. Garnish with fresh lemon wedges.

DIKGOBE (TRIPE AND PEANUT STEW)

Servings: 4

Time: 2 hours

Ingredients:

- 500g tripe, cleaned and cut
- 1 onion, finely chopped
- 2 tomatoes, diced
- 3 cloves garlic, minced
- 1 cup peanuts, ground
- 2 tablespoons vegetable oil
- 1 teaspoon ground coriander
- 1 teaspoon paprika
- 1 teaspoon dried thyme
- 4 cups beef or vegetable broth
- Salt and pepper to taste
- Fresh cilantro for garnish

Instructions:

1. In a large pot, heat vegetable oil over medium heat.
2. Sauté chopped onions until golden brown.
3. Add minced garlic and cook until fragrant.

4. Stir in diced tomatoes, ground peanuts, ground coriander, paprika, and dried thyme.
5. Cook for 3-5 minutes, stirring constantly.
6. Add cleaned and cut tripe to the pot, stirring to coat with the peanut mixture.
7. Pour in beef or vegetable broth, bring to a boil, then reduce heat and simmer for 1.5 to 2 hours until the tripe is tender.
8. Season with salt and pepper to taste.
9. Check the seasoning and adjust if needed.
10. Garnish with fresh cilantro before serving.

MAIN COURSES - VEGETARIAN

TAKA-TAKA (OKRA AND TOMATO STEW)

Servings: 4

Time: 30 minutes

Ingredients:

- 2 cups okra, sliced
- 2 cups tomatoes, chopped
- 1 onion, finely chopped
- 3 cloves garlic, minced
- 2 tablespoons vegetable oil
- 1 teaspoon ground cumin
- 1 teaspoon ground coriander
- 1 teaspoon paprika

- 1 teaspoon dried thyme
- Salt and pepper to taste
- Fresh parsley for garnish

Instructions:

1. In a pan, heat vegetable oil over medium heat.
2. Sauté chopped onions until golden brown.
3. Add minced garlic and cook until fragrant.
4. Stir in chopped tomatoes and cook until they break down.
5. Add sliced okra to the pan, tossing to coat with the tomato mixture.
6. Cook for 10-15 minutes until the okra is tender.
7. Season with ground cumin, ground coriander, paprika, dried thyme, salt, and pepper.
8. Stir thoroughly and cook for an additional 5 minutes.
9. Check the seasoning and adjust if needed.
10. Garnish with fresh parsley before serving.

NHOPI (SWEET POTATO AND PEANUT BUTTER STEW)

Servings: 4

Time: 45 minutes

Ingredients:

- 4 medium-sized sweet potatoes, peeled and diced
- 1 cup creamy peanut butter
- 1 onion, finely chopped
- 2 tomatoes, diced

- 3 cloves garlic, minced
- 2 tablespoons vegetable oil
- 1 teaspoon ground cinnamon
- 1 teaspoon ground nutmeg
- Salt and pepper to taste
- Fresh coriander for garnish

Instructions:

1. In a pot, heat vegetable oil over medium heat.
2. Sauté chopped onions until golden brown.
3. Add minced garlic and cook until fragrant.
4. Stir in diced tomatoes and cook until they break down.
5. Add diced sweet potatoes to the pot, tossing to coat with the tomato mixture.
6. Cook for 10-15 minutes until the sweet potatoes are slightly tender.
7. In a separate bowl, mix peanut butter with a bit of warm water to create a smooth paste.
8. Add the peanut butter paste to the pot, stirring to combine.
9. Season with ground cinnamon, ground nutmeg, salt, and pepper.
10. Simmer for an additional 15-20 minutes until the sweet potatoes are fully cooked and the stew thickens.
11. Check the seasoning and adjust if needed.
12. Garnish with fresh coriander before serving.

MUTAKURA (PUMPKIN AND PEANUT BUTTER STEW)

Servings: 4

Time: 45 minutes

Ingredients:

- 500g pumpkin, peeled and diced
- 1 cup peanut butter
- 1 onion, finely chopped
- 2 tomatoes, diced
- 3 cloves garlic, minced
- 2 tablespoons vegetable oil
- 1 teaspoon ground coriander
- 1 teaspoon paprika
- Salt and pepper to taste
- Fresh parsley for garnish

Instructions:

1. In a pot, heat vegetable oil over medium heat.
2. Sauté chopped onions until golden brown.
3. Add minced garlic and cook until fragrant.
4. Stir in diced tomatoes and cook until they break down.
5. Add diced pumpkin to the pot, tossing to coat with the tomato mixture.
6. Cook for 15-20 minutes until the pumpkin is tender but not mushy.
7. In a bowl, mix peanut butter with a bit of warm water to create a smooth paste.
8. Add the peanut butter paste to the pot, stirring to combine.
9. Season with ground coriander, paprika, salt, and pepper.
10. Simmer for an additional 10-15 minutes until the stew thickens.
11. Check the seasoning and adjust if needed.

12. Garnish with fresh parsley before serving.

CHAKALAKA (SPICY VEGETABLE RELISH)

Servings: 4

Time: 30 minutes

Ingredients:

- 1 onion, finely chopped
- 2 bell peppers, diced (different colors for variety)
- 2 carrots, grated
- 2 tomatoes, diced
- 1 can baked beans in tomato sauce
- 2 tablespoons vegetable oil
- 1 teaspoon curry powder
- 1 teaspoon paprika
- 1 teaspoon ground cumin
- Salt and pepper to taste
- Fresh cilantro for garnish

Instructions:

1. In a pan, heat vegetable oil over medium heat.
2. Sauté chopped onions until soft.
3. Add diced bell peppers and cook until slightly tender.
4. Stir in grated carrots and cook for an additional 3-5 minutes.
5. Add diced tomatoes to the pan and cook until they break down.
6. Pour in baked beans in tomato sauce.

7. Season with curry powder, paprika, ground cumin, salt, and pepper.
8. Simmer the mixture for 10-15 minutes until the vegetables are cooked and flavors meld together.
9. Check the seasoning and adjust if needed.
10. Garnish with fresh cilantro before serving.

MURIWO UNEDOVI (GREENS WITH PEANUT SAUCE)

Servings: 4

Time: 30 minutes

Ingredients:

- 500g mixed greens (collard greens, spinach, or kale), washed and chopped
- 1 cup peanuts, ground
- 1 onion, finely chopped
- 2 tomatoes, diced
- 3 cloves garlic, minced
- 2 tablespoons vegetable oil
- 1 teaspoon ground coriander
- 1 teaspoon paprika
- Salt and pepper to taste
- Fresh lemon wedges for serving

Instructions:

1. In a pot, heat vegetable oil over medium heat.
2. Sauté chopped onions until golden brown.
3. Add minced garlic and cook until fragrant.

4. Stir in diced tomatoes and cook until they break down.
5. Add chopped greens to the pot, tossing to coat with the tomato mixture.
6. Cook for 10-15 minutes until the greens are wilted and tender.
7. In a bowl, mix ground peanuts with a bit of warm water to create a smooth paste.
8. Add the peanut paste to the pot, stirring to combine.
9. Season with ground coriander, paprika, salt, and pepper.
10. Simmer for an additional 5-7 minutes until the greens are cooked through.
11. Check the seasoning and adjust if needed.
12. Serve with fresh lemon wedges on the side.

BAMBARA NUT AND VEGETABLE CURRY

Servings: 4

Time: 45 minutes

Ingredients:

- 1 cup bambara nuts
- 2 cups mixed vegetables (carrots, peas, potatoes)
- 1 onion, finely chopped
- 2 tomatoes, diced
- 3 cloves garlic, minced
- 2 tablespoons vegetable oil
- 1 cup coconut milk
- 2 tablespoons curry powder
- 1 teaspoon ground turmeric
- 1 teaspoon ground cumin
- Salt and pepper to taste

- Fresh cilantro for garnish

Instructions:

1. Rinse bambara nuts under cold water.
2. In a pot, cook bambara nuts in water until tender, following package instructions.
3. In a separate pot, heat vegetable oil over medium heat.
4. Sauté chopped onions until soft.
5. Add minced garlic and cook until fragrant.
6. Stir in diced tomatoes and cook until they break down.
7. Add mixed vegetables to the pot, stirring to coat with the tomato mixture.
8. Pour in coconut milk, curry powder, ground turmeric, and ground cumin.
9. Simmer for 15-20 minutes until the vegetables are cooked through.
10. Add cooked bambara nuts to the pot, stirring gently to combine.
11. Season with salt and pepper to taste.
12. Simmer for an additional 5-7 minutes to allow the flavors to meld.
13. Check the seasoning and adjust if needed.
14. Garnish with fresh cilantro before serving.

MAZHANJE CAKE (BAOBAB FRUIT CAKE)

Servings: 8

Time: 1 hour 15 minutes

Ingredients:

- 2 cups all-purpose flour
- 1 cup baobab fruit pulp (mazhanje), strained
- 1 cup sugar
- 1/2 cup vegetable oil
- 3 eggs
- 1 teaspoon baking powder
- 1/2 teaspoon baking soda
- 1/2 teaspoon vanilla extract
- Pinch of salt
- 1/2 cup chopped nuts (optional, for garnish)
- Powdered sugar for dusting

Instructions:

1. Preheat the oven to 180°C (350°F). Grease and flour a cake pan.
2. In a bowl, sift together flour, baking powder, baking soda, and salt.
3. In a separate bowl, beat together sugar and vegetable oil until creamy.
4. Add eggs one at a time, beating well after each addition.
5. Stir in baobab fruit pulp and vanilla extract.
6. Gradually add the sifted dry ingredients to the wet ingredients, mixing until just combined.
7. Pour the batter into the prepared cake pan.
8. Bake in the preheated oven for 45-50 minutes or until a toothpick inserted into the center comes out clean.
9. Allow the cake to cool in the pan for 10 minutes, then transfer it to a wire rack to cool completely.
10. Once cooled, sprinkle chopped nuts (if using) on top and dust with powdered sugar.

PUMPKIN AND BEAN STEW

Servings: 4

Time: 45 minutes

Ingredients:

- 500g pumpkin, peeled and diced
- 1 can kidney beans, drained and rinsed
- 1 onion, finely chopped
- 2 tomatoes, diced
- 3 cloves garlic, minced
- 2 tablespoons vegetable oil
- 1 teaspoon ground cumin
- 1 teaspoon paprika
- 1 teaspoon dried oregano
- Salt and pepper to taste
- Fresh parsley for garnish

Instructions:

1. In a pot, heat vegetable oil over medium heat.
2. Sauté chopped onions until golden brown.
3. Add minced garlic and cook until fragrant.
4. Stir in diced tomatoes and cook until they break down.
5. Add diced pumpkin to the pot, tossing to coat with the tomato mixture.
6. Cook for 15-20 minutes until the pumpkin is tender but not mushy.
7. Add kidney beans to the pot, stirring gently to combine.
8. Season with ground cumin, paprika, dried oregano, salt, and pepper.
9. Simmer for an additional 10-15 minutes until the stew thickens.

10. Check the seasoning and adjust if needed.
11. Garnish with fresh parsley before serving.

SADZA PATTIES WITH CHIBAGE (BUTTERNUT) SAUCE

Servings: 4

Time: 1 hour

Ingredients: *For Sadza Patties:*

- 2 cups sadza (cornmeal porridge), cooled and solidified
- 1 cup cooked mixed vegetables (peas, carrots, corn), finely chopped
- 1 onion, finely chopped
- 2 tablespoons vegetable oil
- Salt and pepper to taste
- Cooking oil for frying

For Chibage (Butternut) Sauce:

- 2 cups butternut squash, peeled and diced
- 1 onion, finely chopped
- 2 tomatoes, diced
- 3 cloves garlic, minced
- 2 tablespoons vegetable oil
- 1 teaspoon ground coriander
- 1 teaspoon paprika
- Salt and pepper to taste
- Fresh cilantro for garnish

Instructions: *For Sadza Patties:*

1. In a bowl, combine sadza, chopped mixed vegetables, and chopped onions.
2. Season with salt and pepper, then mix well.
3. Shape the mixture into patties.
4. In a pan, heat cooking oil over medium heat.
5. Fry the sadza patties until golden brown on both sides.
6. Remove from the pan and set aside.

For Chibage (Butternut) Sauce:

1. In a pot, heat vegetable oil over medium heat.
2. Sauté chopped onions until soft.
3. Add minced garlic and cook until fragrant.
4. Stir in diced tomatoes and cook until they break down.
5. Add diced butternut squash to the pot, tossing to coat with the tomato mixture.
6. Cook for 20-25 minutes until the butternut squash is tender.
7. Season with ground coriander, paprika, salt, and pepper.
8. Simmer for an additional 5-7 minutes.
9. Check the seasoning and adjust if needed.
10. Serve the Sadza Patties with a generous spoonful of Chibage Sauce.
11. Garnish with fresh cilantro before serving.

MUBOORA AND MUSHROOM PILAF

Servings: 4

Time: 45 minutes

Ingredients:

- 2 cups muboora (pumpkin leaves), chopped
- 1 cup mushrooms, sliced
- 1 cup basmati rice
- 1 onion, finely chopped
- 3 cloves garlic, minced
- 2 tablespoons vegetable oil
- 4 cups vegetable broth
- 1 teaspoon ground turmeric
- 1 teaspoon ground cumin
- Salt and pepper to taste
- Fresh parsley for garnish

Instructions:

1. In a pot, heat vegetable oil over medium heat.
2. Sauté chopped onions until soft.
3. Add minced garlic and cook until fragrant.
4. Stir in sliced mushrooms and cook until they release their moisture.
5. Add chopped muboora (pumpkin leaves) to the pot, tossing to combine.
6. Cook for 10-15 minutes until the vegetables are wilted and tender.
7. Rinse basmati rice under cold water.
8. Add the rice to the pot, stirring to coat with the vegetable mixture.
9. Pour in vegetable broth, ground turmeric, and ground cumin.
10. Season with salt and pepper to taste.
11. Bring the mixture to a boil, then reduce heat to low, cover, and simmer for 20-25 minutes until the rice is cooked and the liquid is absorbed.
12. Fluff the pilaf with a fork.

13. Check the seasoning and adjust if needed.
14. Garnish with fresh parsley before serving.

SIDE DISHES

SADZA (CORNMEAL PORRIDGE)

Servings: 4

Time: 20 minutes

Ingredients:

- 2 cups white cornmeal
- 4 cups water
- Salt to taste

Instructions:

1. In a large pot, bring 4 cups of water to a boil.
2. Gradually add the white cornmeal to the boiling water, stirring continuously to prevent lumps from forming.

3. Reduce the heat to low and continue stirring to ensure a smooth consistency.
4. Cover the pot and let it simmer on low heat for 15-20 minutes, stirring occasionally to prevent sticking.
5. Add salt to taste, adjusting the quantity based on your preference.
6. Continue simmering until the sadza reaches a thick, smooth consistency.
7. Once cooked, remove from heat and allow it to rest for a few minutes before serving.

NHEDZI NADOVI (WILD MUSHROOMS WITH PEANUT BUTTER)

Servings: 4

Time: 30 minutes

Ingredients:

- 2 cups nhedzi (wild mushrooms), cleaned
- 1 onion, finely chopped
- 2 tomatoes, diced
- 3 tablespoons peanut butter
- 2 tablespoons vegetable oil
- 2 cloves garlic, minced
- 1 teaspoon ground coriander
- 1 teaspoon paprika
- Salt and pepper to taste
- Fresh parsley for garnish

Instructions:

1. In a pan, heat vegetable oil over medium heat.
2. Sauté chopped onions until golden brown.
3. Add minced garlic and cook until fragrant.
4. Stir in diced tomatoes and cook until they break down.
5. Add cleaned wild mushrooms (nhedzi) to the pan, tossing to coat with the tomato mixture.
6. Cook for 10-15 minutes until the mushrooms release their moisture.
7. In a small bowl, mix peanut butter with a bit of warm water to create a smooth paste.
8. Add the peanut butter paste to the pan, stirring to combine.
9. Season with ground coriander, paprika, salt, and pepper.
10. Simmer for an additional 5-7 minutes until the sauce thickens and the mushrooms are fully cooked.
11. Check the seasoning and adjust if needed.
12. Garnish with fresh parsley before serving.

HUKU NEDOVI SADZA (CHICKEN WITH PEANUT SAUCE AND CORNMEAL)

Servings: 4

Time: 1 hour

Ingredients: *For Chicken:*

- 1 whole chicken, cut into pieces
- 1 onion, finely chopped
- 2 tomatoes, diced
- 3 tablespoons vegetable oil
- 2 tablespoons groundnut powder (peanut powder)
- 2 cloves garlic, minced

- 1 teaspoon ground coriander
- 1 teaspoon paprika
- Salt and pepper to taste

For Sadza (Cornmeal):

- 2 cups white cornmeal
- 4 cups water
- Salt to taste

Instructions: *For Chicken:*

1. In a large pot, heat vegetable oil over medium heat.
2. Sauté chopped onions until golden brown.
3. Add minced garlic and cook until fragrant.
4. Stir in diced tomatoes and cook until they break down.
5. Add chicken pieces to the pot, browning on all sides.
6. Season with ground coriander, paprika, salt, and pepper.
7. In a small bowl, mix groundnut powder with a bit of warm water to create a smooth paste.
8. Add the groundnut paste to the pot, stirring to combine.
9. Simmer for 30-40 minutes until the chicken is fully cooked and the sauce thickens.
10. Check the seasoning and adjust if needed.

For Sadza (Cornmeal):

1. In a large pot, bring 4 cups of water to a boil.
2. Gradually add the white cornmeal to the boiling water, stirring continuously to prevent lumps.
3. Reduce the heat to low and continue stirring until the sadza reaches a smooth consistency.
4. Cover the pot and let it simmer on low heat for 15-20 minutes, stirring occasionally.

5. Add salt to taste, adjusting the quantity based on your preference.
6. Once cooked, remove from heat and allow it to rest for a few minutes.

MOROGO (WILD SPINACH)

Servings: 4

Time: 20 minutes

Ingredients:

- 4 cups morogo (wild spinach), cleaned and chopped
- 1 onion, finely chopped
- 2 tomatoes, diced
- 2 tablespoons vegetable oil
- 2 cloves garlic, minced
- 1 teaspoon ground coriander
- 1 teaspoon paprika
- Salt and pepper to taste
- Fresh lemon wedges for serving

Instructions:

1. In a pan, heat vegetable oil over medium heat.
2. Sauté chopped onions until golden brown.
3. Add minced garlic and cook until fragrant.
4. Stir in diced tomatoes and cook until they break down.
5. Add cleaned and chopped morogo (wild spinach) to the pan, tossing to coat with the tomato mixture.
6. Cook for 10-15 minutes until the spinach is wilted and tender.

7. Season with ground coriander, paprika, salt, and pepper.
8. Stir thoroughly and cook for an additional 5 minutes.
9. Check the seasoning and adjust if needed.
10. Serve hot with fresh lemon wedges on the side.

DOVI-MAPUTI (PEANUT BRITTLE)

Servings: Approximately 10 pieces

Time: 30 minutes

Ingredients:

- 1 cup roasted peanuts
- 1 cup white sugar
- 1/2 cup water
- 1 tablespoon butter
- 1/2 teaspoon vanilla extract
- 1/4 teaspoon baking soda

Instructions:

1. Prepare a baking sheet by lining it with parchment paper or greasing it with butter.
2. In a dry pan, toast the peanuts over medium heat until they become golden brown. Set aside.
3. In a saucepan, combine sugar and water over medium heat. Stir until the sugar dissolves.
4. Allow the sugar mixture to boil without stirring. Continue boiling until it reaches a light amber color.
5. Carefully stir in the toasted peanuts, butter, and vanilla extract.

6. Continue cooking the mixture until it reaches a rich golden color.
7. Remove the saucepan from heat and quickly stir in the baking soda. The mixture will foam up.
8. Immediately pour the hot mixture onto the prepared baking sheet, spreading it out with a spatula.
9. Allow the Dovi-Maputi to cool and harden completely.
10. Once hardened, break it into pieces or cut it into desired shapes.

MUBOORA AND BUTTERNUT FRITTERS

Servings: 4

Time: 30 minutes

Ingredients:

- 2 cups muboora (pumpkin leaves), finely chopped
- 1 cup butternut squash, grated
- 1 cup all-purpose flour
- 1/2 cup cornmeal
- 1 onion, finely chopped
- 2 tomatoes, diced
- 2 eggs
- 1 teaspoon baking powder
- 1 teaspoon ground coriander
- 1 teaspoon paprika
- Salt and pepper to taste
- Vegetable oil for frying

Instructions:

1. In a bowl, combine chopped muboora, grated butternut squash, all-purpose flour, cornmeal, chopped onions, and diced tomatoes.
2. In a separate bowl, whisk together eggs, baking powder, ground coriander, paprika, salt, and pepper.
3. Pour the egg mixture into the vegetable mixture, stirring until well combined.
4. Heat vegetable oil in a pan over medium heat.
5. Drop spoonfuls of the fritter batter into the hot oil, flattening them slightly with the back of the spoon.
6. Fry the fritters until golden brown on both sides.
7. Remove from the pan and place them on a paper towel to absorb excess oil.
8. Repeat the process until all the batter is used.

MAHEWU BREAD (FERMENTED MAIZE DRINK BREAD)

Servings: 1 loaf

Time: 2 hours

Ingredients:

- 3 cups all-purpose flour
- 1 cup mahewu (fermented maize drink)
- 1/4 cup sugar
- 1/4 cup vegetable oil
- 2 teaspoons active dry yeast
- 1 teaspoon salt
- Additional flour for dusting

Instructions:

1. In a small bowl, combine mahewu and sugar. Stir until the sugar dissolves.
2. Sprinkle the active dry yeast over the mahewu mixture. Let it sit for 5-10 minutes until it becomes frothy.
3. In a large mixing bowl, combine the flour and salt.
4. Make a well in the center of the flour mixture and pour in the yeast-mahewu mixture and vegetable oil.
5. Mix the ingredients to form a dough. Knead the dough on a floured surface for about 10 minutes until it becomes smooth and elastic.
6. Place the dough in a lightly oiled bowl, cover it with a clean kitchen towel, and let it rise in a warm place for 1 hour or until it doubles in size.
7. Preheat the oven to 180°C (350°F).
8. Punch down the risen dough and shape it into a loaf.
9. Place the shaped dough in a greased loaf pan, cover it, and let it rise for an additional 30 minutes.
10. Bake the Mahewu Bread in the preheated oven for 25-30 minutes or until it sounds hollow when tapped on the bottom.
11. Allow the bread to cool before slicing and serving.

PUMPKIN FRITTERS

Servings: 4

Time: 30 minutes

Ingredients:

- 2 cups pumpkin, grated
- 1 cup all-purpose flour
- 1/4 cup sugar

- 2 teaspoons baking powder
- 1/2 teaspoon ground cinnamon
- 1/4 teaspoon ground nutmeg
- 1/4 teaspoon salt
- 2 eggs
- 1/2 cup milk
- Vegetable oil for frying
- Powdered sugar for dusting (optional)

Instructions:

1. In a large bowl, combine grated pumpkin, all-purpose flour, sugar, baking powder, ground cinnamon, ground nutmeg, and salt.
2. In a separate bowl, whisk together eggs and milk.
3. Pour the egg-milk mixture into the pumpkin mixture, stirring until well combined.
4. Heat vegetable oil in a pan over medium heat.
5. Drop spoonfuls of the fritter batter into the hot oil, flattening them slightly with the back of the spoon.
6. Fry the fritters until golden brown on both sides.
7. Remove from the pan and place them on a paper towel to absorb excess oil.
8. Optional: Dust the Pumpkin Fritters with powdered sugar before serving.

NYIMO (BAMBARA NUT) SALAD

Servings: 4

Time: 30 minutes

Ingredients:

- 1 cup nyimo (bambara nuts), cooked and cooled
- 2 cups mixed salad greens (lettuce, spinach, arugula)
- 1 cucumber, sliced
- 1 bell pepper, diced (any color)
- 1 red onion, thinly sliced
- 1 cup cherry tomatoes, halved
- 1/4 cup fresh cilantro, chopped
- 2 tablespoons olive oil
- 1 tablespoon balsamic vinegar
- 1 teaspoon Dijon mustard
- Salt and pepper to taste

Instructions:

1. In a large bowl, combine cooked and cooled nyimo (bambara nuts), mixed salad greens, sliced cucumber, diced bell pepper, thinly sliced red onion, cherry tomatoes, and chopped cilantro.
2. In a small bowl, whisk together olive oil, balsamic vinegar, Dijon mustard, salt, and pepper to create the dressing.
3. Drizzle the dressing over the salad and toss gently to coat the ingredients evenly.
4. Allow the Nyimo Salad to marinate for a few minutes before serving.

CHIBAGE (BUTTERNUT) AND POTATO MASH

Servings: 4

Time: 30 minutes

Ingredients:

- 2 cups chibage (butternut squash), peeled and diced
- 2 cups potatoes, peeled and diced
- 2 tablespoons butter
- 1/4 cup milk
- Salt and pepper to taste
- Fresh parsley for garnish

Instructions:

1. Place diced chibage (butternut squash) and potatoes in a large pot, covering them with water.
2. Bring the pot to a boil and cook the vegetables until they are fork-tender.
3. Drain the cooked chibage and potatoes and return them to the pot.
4. Add butter to the pot and mash the vegetables using a potato masher until smooth.
5. Gradually add milk while continuing to mash until the desired consistency is reached.
6. Season the Chibage and Potato Mash with salt and pepper to taste.
7. Continue mashing and stirring until well combined.
8. Transfer the mash to a serving dish and garnish with fresh parsley.

BREADS AND GRAINS

SADZA LOAF

Servings: 8 slices

Time: 1 hour

Ingredients:

- 2 cups sadza (cornmeal porridge), cooled and solidified
- 1 cup all-purpose flour
- 1 cup buttermilk
- 1/4 cup vegetable oil
- 2 tablespoons sugar
- 1 teaspoon baking powder
- 1/2 teaspoon salt

Instructions:

1. Preheat the oven to 180°C (350°F). Grease and flour a loaf pan.
2. In a large mixing bowl, combine sadza, all-purpose flour, sugar, baking powder, and salt.
3. In a separate bowl, whisk together buttermilk and vegetable oil.
4. Pour the buttermilk mixture into the dry ingredients, stirring until well combined.
5. Transfer the batter into the prepared loaf pan, spreading it evenly.
6. Bake in the preheated oven for 45-50 minutes or until a toothpick inserted into the center comes out clean.
7. Allow the Sadza Loaf to cool in the pan for 10 minutes, then transfer it to a wire rack to cool completely.
8. Once cooled, slice and serve the Sadza Loaf with your favorite spreads or enjoy it as a side to savory dishes.

BOTA-BOTA (TRIPE PORRIDGE)

Servings: 4

Time: 2 hours

Ingredients:

- 2 cups cleaned and diced tripe
- 1 cup sadza (cornmeal)
- 1 onion, finely chopped
- 2 tomatoes, diced
- 3 tablespoons vegetable oil
- 2 cloves garlic, minced

- 1 teaspoon ground coriander
- 1 teaspoon paprika
- Salt and pepper to taste
- Fresh parsley for garnish

Instructions:

1. In a pot, bring 6 cups of water to a boil.
2. Add cleaned and diced tripe to the boiling water. Reduce heat to low and simmer for 1 hour or until the tripe is tender.
3. In a separate bowl, mix sadza with enough water to form a smooth paste.
4. Slowly add the sadza paste to the pot, stirring continuously to avoid lumps.
5. Continue simmering and stirring for an additional 30 minutes, allowing the sadza to thicken the porridge.
6. In a pan, heat vegetable oil over medium heat.
7. Sauté chopped onions until golden brown.
8. Add minced garlic and cook until fragrant.
9. Stir in diced tomatoes and cook until they break down.
10. Add the onion-tomato mixture to the pot of tripe and sadza porridge.
11. Season with ground coriander, paprika, salt, and pepper.
12. Simmer for an additional 15-20 minutes, allowing the flavors to meld.
13. Check the seasoning and adjust if needed.
14. Garnish with fresh parsley before serving.

MAHEWU (FERMENTED MAIZE DRINK)

Servings: 4

Time: 2 days (includes fermentation)

Ingredients:

- 1 cup maize meal
- 4 cups water
- 2 tablespoons sugar
- 1/2 teaspoon salt

Instructions:

1. In a large mixing bowl, combine maize meal, sugar, and salt.
2. Gradually add water to the dry ingredients, stirring continuously to create a smooth, lump-free mixture.
3. Pour the mixture into a clean, airtight container, leaving some space at the top for expansion during fermentation.
4. Seal the container and let it sit at room temperature for 24-48 hours to allow fermentation. The longer it ferments, the tangier the taste will be.
5. After fermentation, strain the Mahewu to remove any solids, using a fine mesh sieve or cheesecloth.
6. Refrigerate the liquid for a few hours until it's well-chilled.
7. Stir the Mahewu before serving to mix any settled particles.

MUPUNGA NENYAMA (RICE AND MEAT)

Servings: 4

Time: 1 hour

Ingredients:

- 2 cups rice, rinsed and drained
- 1 lb beef, cubed
- 1 onion, finely chopped
- 2 tomatoes, diced
- 3 tablespoons vegetable oil
- 2 cups beef or vegetable broth
- 2 teaspoons curry powder
- 1 teaspoon paprika
- 1 teaspoon ground cumin
- Salt and pepper to taste
- Fresh cilantro for garnish

Instructions:

1. In a pot, heat vegetable oil over medium heat.
2. Sauté chopped onions until golden brown.
3. Add cubed beef to the pot, browning on all sides.
4. Stir in diced tomatoes and cook until they break down.
5. Season the meat with curry powder, paprika, ground cumin, salt, and pepper.
6. Pour in beef or vegetable broth, bringing the mixture to a boil.
7. Reduce the heat to low, cover, and simmer for 30-40 minutes or until the meat is tender.
8. In a separate pot, cook the rinsed rice according to package instructions.
9. Once the meat is tender, combine it with the cooked rice, stirring gently to mix.
10. Check the seasoning and adjust if needed.
11. Garnish with fresh cilantro before serving.

MUBOORA MUFFINS

Servings: 12 muffins

Time: 40 minutes

Ingredients:

- 2 cups muboora (pumpkin leaves), finely chopped
- 1 cup all-purpose flour
- 1 cup whole wheat flour
- 1/2 cup vegetable oil
- 1/2 cup milk
- 2 eggs
- 1 cup grated cheddar cheese
- 1 onion, finely chopped
- 2 teaspoons baking powder
- 1 teaspoon salt
- 1/2 teaspoon black pepper
- 1/2 teaspoon paprika
- Fresh parsley for garnish

Instructions:

1. Preheat the oven to 180°C (350°F). Grease a muffin tin or line it with paper liners.
2. In a large mixing bowl, combine all-purpose flour, whole wheat flour, baking powder, salt, black pepper, and paprika.
3. In a separate bowl, whisk together vegetable oil, milk, and eggs.
4. Pour the wet ingredients into the dry ingredients, stirring until just combined.

5. Fold in the chopped muboora, grated cheddar cheese, and chopped onion into the batter.
6. Spoon the batter into the prepared muffin tin, filling each cup about two-thirds full.
7. Bake in the preheated oven for 20-25 minutes or until a toothpick inserted into the center of a muffin comes out clean.
8. Allow the Muboora Muffins to cool in the tin for 5 minutes, then transfer them to a wire rack to cool completely.
9. Garnish with fresh parsley before serving.

SORGHUM AND MILLET PORRIDGE

Servings: 4

Time: 30 minutes

Ingredients:

- 1 cup sorghum grains
- 1 cup millet grains
- 4 cups water
- 2 tablespoons sugar (optional)
- Pinch of salt
- Milk or yogurt for serving
- Fresh fruit for topping (e.g., bananas, berries)

Instructions:

1. In a fine-mesh sieve, rinse the sorghum and millet grains under cold water.
2. In a large pot, combine sorghum, millet, and water.

3. Bring the mixture to a boil over medium-high heat.
4. Reduce the heat to low, cover the pot, and simmer for 20-25 minutes or until the grains are tender. Stir occasionally to prevent sticking.
5. If desired, add sugar and a pinch of salt, adjusting to taste.
6. Continue simmering for an additional 5 minutes to allow the flavors to meld.
7. Remove the pot from heat and let the porridge rest for a few minutes.
8. Serve the Sorghum and Millet Porridge warm, topped with milk or yogurt and fresh fruit.

PUMPKIN BREAD

Servings: 10 slices

Time: 1 hour 15 minutes

Ingredients:

- 1 3/4 cups all-purpose flour
- 1 teaspoon baking soda
- 1/2 teaspoon baking powder
- 1/2 teaspoon salt
- 1 teaspoon ground cinnamon
- 1/2 teaspoon ground nutmeg
- 1/4 teaspoon ground cloves
- 1/2 cup unsalted butter, softened
- 1 cup granulated sugar
- 2 large eggs
- 1 cup canned pumpkin puree
- 1/4 cup milk

- 1 teaspoon vanilla extract
- 1/2 cup chopped nuts (optional)

Instructions:

1. Preheat the oven to 350°F (175°C). Grease and flour a 9x5-inch loaf pan.
2. In a medium bowl, whisk together the flour, baking soda, baking powder, salt, cinnamon, nutmeg, and cloves.
3. In a large bowl, cream together the softened butter and granulated sugar until light and fluffy.
4. Beat in the eggs one at a time, ensuring each is fully incorporated.
5. Add the pumpkin puree, milk, and vanilla extract to the wet ingredients. Mix until well combined.
6. Gradually add the dry ingredients to the wet ingredients, mixing until just combined. Do not overmix.
7. If using nuts, fold them into the batter.
8. Pour the batter into the prepared loaf pan, spreading it evenly.
9. Bake in the preheated oven for 60-70 minutes or until a toothpick inserted into the center comes out clean.
10. Allow the Pumpkin Bread to cool in the pan for 10 minutes, then transfer it to a wire rack to cool completely.

TSUNGA (FINGER MILLET) PANCAKES

Servings: 4

Time: 30 minutes

Ingredients:

- 1 cup tsunga (finger millet) flour
- 1/2 cup all-purpose flour
- 2 tablespoons sugar
- 1 teaspoon baking powder
- 1/2 teaspoon salt
- 1 cup milk
- 1 egg
- 2 tablespoons melted butter
- Butter or oil for cooking
- Honey or syrup for serving

Instructions:

1. In a large mixing bowl, combine tsunga flour, all-purpose flour, sugar, baking powder, and salt.
2. In a separate bowl, whisk together milk, egg, and melted butter.
3. Pour the wet ingredients into the dry ingredients, stirring until just combined. The batter may be slightly lumpy.
4. Heat a griddle or non-stick skillet over medium heat and add a small amount of butter or oil.
5. Pour 1/4 cup portions of batter onto the hot griddle, spreading it slightly with the back of a spoon to form pancakes.
6. Cook until bubbles form on the surface, then flip and cook the other side until golden brown.
7. Repeat with the remaining batter, adding more butter or oil as needed.
8. Serve the Tsunga Pancakes warm, drizzled with honey or syrup.

SADZA CAKES WITH GREENS

Servings: 4

Time: 45 minutes

Ingredients:

- 2 cups sadza (cornmeal porridge), cooled and solidified
- 1 cup mixed greens (collard greens, kale, or spinach), finely chopped
- 1 onion, finely chopped
- 2 tomatoes, diced
- 2 tablespoons vegetable oil
- 2 cloves garlic, minced
- 1 teaspoon ground coriander
- 1 teaspoon paprika
- Salt and pepper to taste
- Cooking oil for frying

Instructions:

1. In a large bowl, crumble the cooled and solidified sadza into small pieces.
2. In a pan, heat vegetable oil over medium heat.
3. Sauté chopped onions until golden brown.
4. Add minced garlic and cook until fragrant.
5. Stir in diced tomatoes and cook until they break down.
6. Add the finely chopped mixed greens to the pan, tossing to coat with the onion-tomato mixture. Cook until the greens are wilted.
7. Season with ground coriander, paprika, salt, and pepper. Stir thoroughly.
8. Add the sautéed greens mixture to the crumbled sadza, combining well to form a uniform mixture.

9. Shape the mixture into small cakes or patties.
10. Heat cooking oil in a skillet over medium-high heat.
11. Fry the Sadza Cakes until golden brown on both sides.
12. Remove from the skillet and place on a paper towel to absorb excess oil.

BAMBARA NUT PORRIDGE

Servings: 4

Time: 45 minutes

Ingredients:

- 1 cup bambara nuts
- 4 cups water
- 2 cups milk
- 1/4 cup sugar (adjust to taste)
- 1/4 teaspoon ground cinnamon
- 1/4 teaspoon vanilla extract
- Pinch of salt
- Chopped nuts or dried fruit for garnish (optional)

Instructions:

1. Rinse the bambara nuts under cold water to remove any dirt or debris.
2. In a pot, combine bambara nuts and water. Bring to a boil over medium-high heat.
3. Reduce the heat to low, cover the pot, and simmer for 30-40 minutes or until the bambara nuts are tender. Stir occasionally.

4. Once the bambara nuts are tender, drain any excess water.
5. In a blender, combine the cooked bambara nuts with milk, sugar, ground cinnamon, vanilla extract, and a pinch of salt.
6. Blend until smooth and creamy.
7. Pour the blended mixture back into the pot and heat over low heat, stirring continuously until the porridge reaches your desired consistency.
8. Adjust the sweetness to taste by adding more sugar if necessary.
9. Remove from heat and let the Bambara Nut Porridge cool slightly before serving.
10. Garnish with chopped nuts or dried fruit if desired.

DESSERTS AND SWEETS

MAHEU ICE CREAM

Servings: 6

Time: 6 hours (includes freezing time)

Ingredients:

- 2 cups maheu (fermented maize drink)
- 1 cup heavy cream
- 1/2 cup condensed milk
- 1 teaspoon vanilla extract
- Pinch of salt

Instructions:

1. In a mixing bowl, combine maheu, heavy cream, condensed milk, vanilla extract, and a pinch of salt.
2. Whisk the ingredients together until well combined.
3. Pour the mixture into an ice cream maker and churn according to the manufacturer's instructions.
4. Once the ice cream reaches a soft-serve consistency, transfer it to a lidded container.
5. Freeze the Maheu Ice Cream for at least 4-6 hours or until firm.
6. Before serving, let the ice cream sit at room temperature for a few minutes to soften slightly.

MAPOPO (GUAVA) SORBET

Servings: 4

Time: 4 hours (includes freezing time)

Ingredients:

- 4 cups guava juice (freshly squeezed or store-bought)
- 1/2 cup sugar (adjust to taste)
- 2 tablespoons fresh lime or lemon juice
- Zest of one lime or lemon (optional)

Instructions:

1. In a mixing bowl, combine guava juice and sugar, stirring until the sugar dissolves.
2. Add fresh lime or lemon juice to the guava mixture and stir well.
3. Taste the mixture and adjust the sweetness by adding more sugar if necessary.

4. If using, stir in the lime or lemon zest for an extra burst of citrus flavor.
5. Pour the guava mixture into a shallow, lidded container, ensuring it's spread evenly.
6. Place the container in the freezer and let it set for about 2 hours.
7. After 2 hours, use a fork to break up any ice crystals that may have formed.
8. Repeat this process every hour for the next 2-3 hours until the sorbet reaches the desired consistency.
9. Once fully frozen and firm, the Mapopo Sorbet is ready to be scooped and served.

DOVI PUDDING

Servings: 6

Time: 1 hour

Ingredients:

- 1 cup peanut butter
- 1 cup sugar
- 1/2 cup maize meal
- 4 cups water
- 1 teaspoon vanilla extract
- Pinch of salt
- Ground cinnamon for garnish (optional)

Instructions:

1. In a mixing bowl, whisk together peanut butter, sugar, maize meal, and water until well combined.

2. Pour the mixture into a pot and place it over medium heat.
3. Stir continuously to prevent lumps from forming, and bring the mixture to a gentle boil.
4. Reduce the heat to low and let it simmer for 30-40 minutes, stirring regularly until the pudding thickens.
5. Add vanilla extract and a pinch of salt, stirring to incorporate.
6. Once the Dovi Pudding reaches a smooth and creamy consistency, remove it from heat.
7. Allow the pudding to cool for a few minutes before serving.
8. Optionally, sprinkle ground cinnamon on top for extra flavor and presentation.

MBATATA (SWEET POTATO) PIE

Servings: 8

Time: 1 hour 30 minutes

Ingredients:

For the Crust:

- 1 1/2 cups all-purpose flour
- 1/2 cup unsalted butter, chilled and cubed
- 1/4 cup granulated sugar
- Pinch of salt
- 3-4 tablespoons cold water

For the Filling:

- 2 cups mashed mbatata (sweet potatoes)
- 1/2 cup brown sugar, packed
- 1/4 cup unsalted butter, melted
- 1/2 cup evaporated milk
- 2 large eggs
- 1 teaspoon vanilla extract
- 1/2 teaspoon ground cinnamon
- 1/4 teaspoon ground nutmeg
- 1/4 teaspoon salt

Instructions:

For the Crust:

1. In a food processor, combine all-purpose flour, chilled and cubed butter, granulated sugar, and a pinch of salt.
2. Pulse until the mixture resembles coarse crumbs.
3. Gradually add cold water, one tablespoon at a time, pulsing until the dough comes together.
4. Turn the dough out onto a lightly floured surface and shape it into a disc.
5. Wrap the dough in plastic wrap and refrigerate for at least 30 minutes.
6. Preheat the oven to 375°F (190°C).

For the Filling:

1. In a large bowl, combine mashed mbatata, brown sugar, melted butter, evaporated milk, eggs, vanilla extract, ground cinnamon, ground nutmeg, and salt.
2. Mix until well combined and smooth.

Assembling the Pie:

1. Roll out the chilled dough on a floured surface to fit a 9-inch pie dish.
2. Carefully transfer the rolled-out dough to the pie dish, pressing it against the bottom and sides.
3. Trim any excess dough and crimp the edges.
4. Pour the sweet potato filling into the prepared pie crust, spreading it evenly.
5. Bake in the preheated oven for 45-50 minutes or until the center is set and the crust is golden brown.
6. Allow the Mbatata Pie to cool before slicing and serving.

BANANA FRITTERS

Servings: 4

Time: 30 minutes

Ingredients:

- 4 ripe bananas, mashed
- 1 cup all-purpose flour
- 2 tablespoons sugar
- 1 teaspoon baking powder
- 1/2 teaspoon ground cinnamon
- 1/4 teaspoon salt
- 1/2 cup milk
- 1 teaspoon vanilla extract
- Cooking oil for frying
- Powdered sugar for dusting (optional)

Instructions:

1. In a large mixing bowl, combine mashed bananas, all-purpose flour, sugar, baking powder, ground cinnamon, and salt.
2. In a separate bowl, whisk together milk and vanilla extract.
3. Gradually add the wet ingredients to the banana mixture, stirring until a thick batter forms.
4. Heat cooking oil in a deep skillet or frying pan over medium heat.
5. Once the oil is hot, drop spoonfuls of the banana batter into the oil, making small fritters.
6. Fry the banana fritters for 2-3 minutes on each side or until golden brown and cooked through.
7. Use a slotted spoon to remove the fritters from the oil and place them on a paper towel to absorb excess oil.
8. If desired, dust the banana fritters with powdered sugar before serving.

MAZIWA MALAMBE (CONDENSED MILK FUDGE)

Servings: 20 pieces

Time: 1 hour (plus cooling time)

Ingredients:

- 2 cups sweetened condensed milk
- 1/2 cup unsalted butter
- 1 cup brown sugar
- 1 teaspoon vanilla extract
- Pinch of salt

- Chopped nuts or desiccated coconut for coating (optional)

Instructions:

1. In a non-stick saucepan, combine sweetened condensed milk, unsalted butter, brown sugar, vanilla extract, and a pinch of salt.
2. Place the saucepan over medium heat, stirring continuously to prevent burning.
3. Continue cooking and stirring until the mixture thickens and starts to pull away from the sides of the pan. This should take about 15-20 minutes.
4. Remove the saucepan from heat and let the mixture cool slightly.
5. Once the mixture is cool enough to handle, grease your hands with a little butter or oil.
6. Take small portions of the mixture and roll them into bite-sized balls or shape them into squares.
7. If desired, roll the fudge pieces in chopped nuts or desiccated coconut to coat them.
8. Place the shaped fudge on a parchment paper-lined tray to cool completely.
9. Allow the Maziwa Malambe to set for a few hours or overnight.
10. Once set, store the fudge in an airtight container at room temperature.

MAHEWU SMOOTHIE

Servings: 2

Time: 10 minutes

Ingredients:

- 1 cup mahewu (fermented maize drink)
- 1 ripe banana
- 1/2 cup plain yogurt
- 1/2 cup mixed berries (strawberries, blueberries, raspberries)
- 1 tablespoon honey (optional)
- Ice cubes (optional)

Instructions:

1. In a blender, combine mahewu, ripe banana, plain yogurt, mixed berries, and honey.
2. Blend the ingredients until smooth and creamy.
3. If a colder smoothie is desired, add ice cubes and blend until the desired consistency is reached.
4. Taste the smoothie and adjust sweetness by adding more honey if necessary.
5. Pour the Mahewu Smoothie into glasses and serve immediately.

MUTAKURA (PUMPKIN) DOUGHNUTS

Servings: 12 doughnuts

Time: 1 hour (plus resting time)

Ingredients:

For the Doughnuts:

- 1 cup cooked and mashed mutakura (pumpkin)

- 3 cups all-purpose flour
- 1/2 cup sugar
- 1 teaspoon baking powder
- 1/2 teaspoon baking soda
- 1/2 teaspoon ground cinnamon
- 1/4 teaspoon ground nutmeg
- 1/4 teaspoon salt
- 1/2 cup buttermilk
- 1 large egg
- 2 tablespoons unsalted butter, melted
- Vegetable oil for frying

For the Coating:

- 1/2 cup sugar
- 1 teaspoon ground cinnamon

Instructions:

1. In a large mixing bowl, combine mashed mutakura, all-purpose flour, sugar, baking powder, baking soda, ground cinnamon, ground nutmeg, and salt.
2. In a separate bowl, whisk together buttermilk, egg, and melted butter.
3. Pour the wet ingredients into the dry ingredients, stirring until a soft dough forms.
4. Turn the dough out onto a floured surface and knead gently until smooth.
5. Cover the dough and let it rest for 30 minutes.
6. Roll out the rested dough to a thickness of about 1/2 inch.
7. Use a doughnut cutter or a round cookie cutter to cut out doughnuts and place them on a floured surface.

8. Heat vegetable oil in a deep fryer or large, deep skillet to 350°F (175°C).
9. Fry the doughnuts in batches, turning them until golden brown on both sides.
10. Remove the fried doughnuts and place them on a paper towel to absorb excess oil.
11. In a shallow bowl, combine sugar and ground cinnamon for the coating.
12. While the doughnuts are still warm, roll them in the sugar-cinnamon mixture to coat evenly.
13. Allow the Mutakura Doughnuts to cool slightly before serving.

CHIBAGE (BUTTERNUT) MUFFINS

Servings: 12 muffins

Time: 40 minutes

Ingredients:

- 1 cup butternut squash, cooked and mashed
- 2 cups all-purpose flour
- 1/2 cup sugar
- 2 teaspoons baking powder
- 1/2 teaspoon baking soda
- 1/2 teaspoon ground cinnamon
- 1/4 teaspoon ground nutmeg
- 1/4 teaspoon salt
- 2 large eggs
- 1/2 cup vegetable oil
- 1/2 cup milk
- 1 teaspoon vanilla extract

- Chopped nuts or raisins for garnish (optional)

Instructions:

1. Preheat the oven to 375°F (190°C). Line a muffin tin with paper liners or grease the cups.
2. In a large mixing bowl, combine mashed butternut squash, all-purpose flour, sugar, baking powder, baking soda, ground cinnamon, ground nutmeg, and salt.
3. In a separate bowl, whisk together eggs, vegetable oil, milk, and vanilla extract.
4. Pour the wet ingredients into the dry ingredients, stirring until just combined. Do not overmix.
5. Spoon the batter into the prepared muffin tin, filling each cup about two-thirds full.
6. If desired, sprinkle chopped nuts or raisins on top of each muffin for garnish.
7. Bake in the preheated oven for 18-20 minutes or until a toothpick inserted into the center of a muffin comes out clean.
8. Allow the Chibage Muffins to cool in the tin for 5 minutes, then transfer them to a wire rack to cool completely.

MADORA (CATERPILLAR) CHOCOLATE TRUFFLES

Servings: 20 truffles

Time: 1 hour (plus chilling time)

Ingredients:

- 1 cup madora (caterpillars), cleaned and roasted
- 1 cup dark chocolate, chopped
- 1/2 cup heavy cream
- 2 tablespoons unsalted butter
- 1/4 cup cocoa powder (for coating)
- Chopped nuts or shredded coconut for coating (optional)

Instructions:

1. In a food processor, pulse the roasted madora until finely ground.
2. In a heatproof bowl, combine the chopped dark chocolate, heavy cream, and unsalted butter.
3. Melt the chocolate mixture using a double boiler or by microwaving in short intervals, stirring until smooth.
4. Stir the ground madora into the melted chocolate mixture until well combined.
5. Cover the bowl with plastic wrap and refrigerate for at least 2 hours or until the mixture is firm enough to handle.
6. Once chilled, scoop small portions of the mixture and roll them into bite-sized truffles.
7. In a shallow dish, combine cocoa powder (and chopped nuts or shredded coconut if using) for coating.
8. Roll each truffle in the coating mixture until evenly covered.
9. Place the coated truffles on a parchment paper-lined tray and refrigerate for an additional 30 minutes to set.
10. Serve the Madora Chocolate Truffles chilled and enjoy the unique blend of caterpillars and rich chocolate!

MEASUREMENT CONVERSIONS

Volume Conversions:

- 1 cup = 8 fluid ounces = 240 milliliters
- 1 tablespoon = 3 teaspoons = 15 milliliters
- 1 fluid ounce = 2 tablespoons = 30 milliliters
- 1 quart = 4 cups = 32 fluid ounces = 946 milliliters
- 1 gallon = 4 quarts = 128 fluid ounces = 3.78 liters
- 1 liter = 1,000 milliliters = 33.8 fluid ounces
- 1 milliliter = 0.034 fluid ounces = 0.002 cups

Weight Conversions:

- 1 pound = 16 ounces = 453.592 grams
- 1 ounce = 28.349 grams
- 1 gram = 0.035 ounces = 0.001 kilograms
- 1 kilogram = 1,000 grams = 35.274 ounces = 2.205 pounds

Temperature Conversions:

- To convert from Fahrenheit to Celsius: (°F - 32) / 1.8
- To convert from Celsius to Fahrenheit: (°C * 1.8) + 32

Length Conversions:

- 1 inch = 2.54 centimeters
- 1 foot = 12 inches = 30.48 centimeters
- 1 yard = 3 feet = 36 inches = 91.44 centimeters
- 1 meter = 100 centimeters = 1.094 yards.

Printed in Great Britain
by Amazon